First published in Great Britain in 1997 by
POETRY NOW
1-2 Wainman Road, Woodston,
Peterborough, PE2 7BU
Telephone (01733) 230746
Fax (01733) 230751

HB ISBN 1 86188 791 4
SB ISBN 1 86188 796 5

FOREWORD

Although we are a nation of poetry writers we are accused of not reading poetry and not buying poetry books: after many years of listening to the incessant gripes of poetry publishers, I can only assume that the books they publish, in general, are books that most people do not want to read.

Poetry should not be obscure, introverted, and as cryptic as a crossword puzzle: it is the poet's duty to reach out and embrace the world.

The world owes the poet nothing and we should not be expected to dig and delve into a rambling discourse searching for some inner meaning.

The reason we write poetry (and almost all of us do) is because we want to communicate: an ideal; an idea; or a specific feeling. Poetry is as essential in communication, as a letter; a radio; a telephone, and the main criteria for selecting the poems in this anthology is very simple: they communicate.

Poetry Now Yorkshire 1998 represents a new set of voices; a flourishing generation of poets in a new landmark in anthologies of modern poetry.

The poems inside have been selected because they communicate directly to the reader. The poets have been inspired by many modern day issues yet many have simply been inspired by life. The intricacies of human life constantly fascinate us, poetry provides an opportunity to unravel our own personalities and view things from different perspectives.

This collection is varied and innovative but it will grab the readers' interest from the first page to the last.

CONTENTS

THE ANGEL'S SONG

The eyes once bright are dimmer now
And the smile seems sad somehow
The sigh I once took for being content
Now doesn't convey what it once meant.

The hunger for adventure has burnt out
The assured walk now full of doubt
And the hands once slender and strong
Twists and turns as if doing wrong

The age of youth a fickle thought
Time its careless sorrow has brought
Memories mean nothing if living has gone
With the only clear sound, the angel's song.

Hazel Graham

EARTH'S NEW BIRTH

Earth's busy season
re-birth and growth
light and warmth
and lengthening days
warm winds
glorious dawns
blue skies
nature's greenness
blossomed trees
tall grasses
scented hedgerows
and delicate flora.

Movement and sounds
smells of freshness
birds constant chorus
insects humming
white woolly lambs
spindly legged calves
planting and sowing
tractors mowing.

Unshuttered windows
tubs filled with colour
people smiling
girls in bright dresses
dancing footsteps
heads held high
laughter and music
and welcoming arms.

Sylvia Suddes

AUTUMN LOVE

Like the golden flames of autumn, does my love burn bright for you,
While in deep those glowing embers, will each day my love renew,
For every crimson dawn that greets thee, for every star that shines
the night,
Does my heart beseech thee, let not your love take flight,
In the heat of night when oft I wake in our tangled warm embrace,
Dare I not tempt to breath, lest will go the smile that rests upon
your face,
Nor dare I make to move, that this might break the spell,
So still I lay in chance to prove, with words no sage could tell,
Of this fire that burns within me, consuming every fear,
When comes the time dawn will wake, and you no longer near,
What chance then my sleepless dreams, that you would make
come true,
Will they then in ashes end, those vows we made when love was new,
For your love, like the autumn sun, sheds now its golden light,
And those golden days now in darkness live, in winter's never-ending
night.
But deep in my heart the smoke still lingers, feeding the spark of
hope and pain,
That will light once more the fire within me,
Should in dreams perchance I meet my autumn love again.

Jim Cuthbert

LOVE DOES STRANGE THINGS

Love has the power,
to make you heart bleed,
especially if it's someone,
someone you need.

Love is something,
no-one can explain,
it can be exciting,
but it always leads to pain.

When it finally hits you,
there's nothing you can do,
your heart is broken,
it's something you've got to get through.

I gave it all,
all I could give,
my heart's bleeding,
but I'll live.

Charlene Potter (15)

FRIENDSHIP

Friendship is like a bed of roses,
or a field of dappled horses.
Two people sharing -
helping and caring.
Someone who's always there -
two friends are - a special pair.
Listening to problems
and taking advice.
You can't buy friendship
there could never be a price.
You'll always have friends
no matter what
they don't just leave
like the latest trends.
They're there to talk to
and confide in -
you'll sometimes argue,
but don't worry
arguing's not a sin.

Heidi Beth Davies

UNDERSTANDING

The bracken was turning brown,
The grass all covered in dew,
He spotted them high on a hillside,
A bleating lamb and a ewe.

His view was obstructed by bracken
It was head high - and higher in places,
But his master's whistles he knew by heart,
And a direct path he traces.

Such is his faith in his master,
Together they work as one.
He asks no greater reward,
Than a pat and a friendly 'well done'.

C V Dewdney

Summer In Swaledale

Rugged hills,
grey crazed rocks,
sheep bitten turf
burnt golden brown.
Sun bleached boulders
border the Swale,
a mere cool trickle
of its winter self.

Cool leafy lanes
shot by cerise fireweed,
steeped in spicy honeysuckle.
Scarlet poppies shine
through fields of golden grain.
Suspended trill of skylark
pervades the atmosphere -
in Swaledale - in summer.

Betty Robertson

WITNESSES

Fragmented lives scattered about
Sharp-edged as broken mirror glass,
Memories of harms done, physical injuries,
Wonderment at threats, and monumental cowardice.

Where did this marriage go to?
Down life's fast track at ninety mph
With carriages of laughing people
Who, later, would conceive children?

Why did its spectacular de-railing
With such huge loss of innocent imaginings.
Go as unreported as a dog's death,
As unremarked as a pauper's funeral?

When did this harsh shouting start?
Those fearful bruising confrontations?
Words as detonators and explosives
Designed to demolish buildings, ruin lives.

In the midst of life's collapsing brickwork,
Isolated as single screams,
Children stand as witnesses
To unnatural selection, and the end of dreams.

David Bramley

DESTINY

The distance is essential.
Compulsory space between life-forms,
Intimacy shattered;
Before the memory of childlike ideas.

Tears pour like wine from the pupil of hope,
Carrying the illusion that they'll ease the torment.
Bitterness stains the oxygen around them
As the discovery of difference is made.

The inevitable fate lies ahead,
Sitting inches from the hypocritical pair.
Kisses lost in mutual suicide;
Voluntarily erased within a single mind.

Liz Fisher

THE DARK CONTINENT

The envelope of the dark continent yawns
and armed with sixty magic secrets I mount
the canon against the storm where as witness
we hear the clanking prison door,
questioned like common criminals to the reason
of the tyranny of another day,
but alas the praise and mortal glory of this old
world can heap upon measure its poets Breton has
left yet unabandoned with an empty skull whose tongue
has turned to salty ash to speak no more,
or whose eyes do not fasten on to the splendour
of our dreams;
his voice still can be heard above the wind,
the deep black forest or the course we charter
weeping through the stars or the dark night
of the soul . . .

Benjamin Flower

YOU ARE A STAR

You are a star that shines so bright
up in the sky that holy night
you shine so strong, you make me cry
for you left me oh so soon you died.
To mourn and weep for your soul
your memory I am proud to own
but on that cold night, not so long ago
when they took away your heart and soul
they took my heart along with yours
so we can be together
heart and soul as one
you are my friend forever.

Sue Owen

CONFLICT

Soldiers parading on the square
Aeroplanes flying in the air
Navy ships out at sea
Come, sit upon my knee.

Now you're comfy my story can begin
I'll tell about a war the British did win
It was on an island out in the sea
So cold and dark you could not see.

Argentinian soldiers were everywhere
They gave the Falkland islanders a terrible scare
This island belongs to Britain
Who would not be beaten into submission.

In went our Navy, Airforce, Army too
They caused one heck of a hullabaloo
The Royal Marines marched over mountains and hill
Came across Argentinians they had to kill.

Out on the sea battleships were sunk
At the time sailors were asleep in their bunk
Aeroplanes screamed across the sky
As their pilots sat and watched their bombs fly.

Oh dear what a terrible war
Soldiers with feet swollen and sore
Then came the day the battle was won
Our brave British forces could relax in the sun.

Ray Jacks

THE NILE CRUISE

The Aurara is a paddle steamer sailing down the Nile
With blue skies and calm seas the long days to while.
The Felucca boats beside the bank bob up and down with glee
at such a majestic sight the cruise boat can be

We dock at dawn and go ashore to see the many things
the temples, and the palaces, the Valleys of the Kings.
A Calesh we must take ride in and see the Winter Palace
the markets and the Monuments, oh what a lot of Hassle.

The traders shout and call you they never get fed up
A barter here! A Bakeesh there! A tablecloth, a cup.
The Bazaars are busy places, with shops by the mile
but everywhere you go to, you are greeted with a smile.

The pyramids of Gizza, the Sphinx, the Great High dam
Egypt and its treasures are everything that can
be seen as life's wonders like King Tutankhamen's Tomb
The Temples of Ramses, and Goddesses of the Sun.

The many wonders surround us, the people and the art
Their culture, intermingled with our luxury and part
of all their friendliness rubs off against us as acquaintances are made
pictures taken, names exchanged, and the return journey is relayed.

Plans to come again maybe, when the temperatures are cool.
The sun beats down and the time has come to jump into the pool.
The ship turns round and blows her horn the return journey has begun,
Then it's goodbye to the crew and friends, the wonders and the sun.

Sheila Storr

THE MISTS OF TIME

Richmond Castle, through the mists of time,
Casting your long shadow over the ancient town.
Forever guarding your secrets in days of renown.

Your great Norman keep, so strong and tall,
Still keeping the watch over crumbling wall.

If those stone walls could wake and speak,
What wondrous tales would they tell?
Of battles and knights of old,
Their fortunes come to seek.

Could the ghost of Earl Alan still walk in the tower
And what was that shadow flitting in the misty bower?

Will King Arthur and his knights
Ever rise to the trumpet's last call?
To save this fair land and rule over all.

Should the little drummer boy in the tunnel dark
Give his last ghostly moan when he reaches his mark?

Magic and mystery dwells in your walls
As you stand like a sentinel's tall prime,
Your secrets will stand for ever safe
Through all the mists of time.

Edith Sunter

PARENTS

Why do parents always know best?
And so in the winter
They make you wear a thermal vest.
Why do parents always know best?

Why do parents think they know best?
And they always think you look lovely
In a Sunday dress.
Why do parents think they know best?

Why is it that parents know best?
And you only realise it
When you become
Parentless!

Emma Dawn Loftus

BELATED THOUGHTS

I wish with all my heart
that we can make a new start in life
I wish I could have seen the pain
all those years ago
when I was a selfish man
with only one plan in life
to enjoy myself.
Please try to understand
words and thoughts
of better things, cloud minds.
I wish once again I could hold you
in the palm of my hand
and make you realise
my new plan in life is you.

June Smith

Hidden Shadows Wait For You . . .

Darkness falls.
Shadows hide.
Dreams will live,
Reality will die.

Blood is life.
Drink my blood.
Darkness falls,
Death to good.

Garlic poison.
Sunlight kills.
A hearty stake,
Christian wills.

The cross will fall,
Darkness rises.
Drain the life,
Drink my blood.

The end will come,
When teeth drip blood,
The passion of poison,
Is feeling the bite.
Join us, the darkness,
Be blood life.

Forget reality,

End your strife.

Turn to a living death.

End your life.

Marie Akers

BLOWING

The north wind blowing, fierce and strong,
snatching words, scattering leaves,
nudging puffball clouds along,
breaking blossoms, bending trees.
Wild in voice with powerful grasp,
seizing, lifting, out to kill
until the evening's final gasp
you linger, falter, sombre, still.

Blowing on the trail of time
my thoughts, like leaves, are flown away,
do they reach that love of mine
or do they die at close of day?
Blowing always, hunger-tossed,
wanting, needing, now I know
the depth of love I nearly lost,
the truth of love that can but grow.

Blowing are my longings now
to breach the tortured wind I try,
in its fervour stay unbowed
and look it coldly in the eye.
I'll whisper gently on the breeze,
send kisses soft as thistledown,
and see lover's spiral, like the leaves,
rise up and circle round and round.

Ann Rutherford

THE FEATHER BOA CONSTRICTOR

Do they know what it is to love?
Or do they feel nothing but lust?

They see their prey across the room.
They watch and wait.
But for their prey it's already too late.
Then they pounce.
It's a game of cat and mouse.
Close together on the dance floor.
They drape round their victim's neck
Like a feather boa constrictor.
And that's when they go in for the kill.
So stay away from them.
Because their kind of love,
Is such a lethal pill.

Rachel C Zaino

AUTUMN TERM

I have watched the first leaves fall
And known the chilly consciousness
Of shedded years
Time blown away
Gone from my keeping now.
I see the placid lake
Its greyness streaked with gold
And try to let its stillness
Permeate my soul.
Maturing wisdom
Bids me slow my pace
To gather treasure from the moments
As some seek
The fruit of hedgerows
Autumn's berried store.
The larder of my memory
Has room enough
For yet more taking in
Of nature's gifts
To nurture coming winter's
Leaner stock.

Cloud-piercing
Sunlit hope
Breaks through,
Reminding me of life's
Immeasurable time-span
Yet to be,
The beckoning reaches
Of eternity
Much closer now.

Eileen Williams

THE DISHFORTH TREES

Long ago, when the hangar was new,
It must have looked bare and ugly
So someone brought trees.
Little trees, selected with care,
Brought and planted to make the airfield like home.

Home it was to Canadian lads
Brought by the winds of war
To fly out of here.
As the storm clouds stretched across Europe
For six long years, the little trees grew;
Each spring, their bright new leaves
Brought hope.

Peacetime, and the trees grew big;
The bombers left, the Canadian lads flew away.
The hangar became the home
Of gliders, the trees became the homes
Of birds.

Then the Army moved in.
The hangars were looking too homely.
The birds had to go.
And the beautiful Dishforth trees,
The trees which had welcomed the bombers back,
Bright leaves just reaching their peaceful prime,
Were chopped.

Jill Povall

MAID OF THE MIST (NIAGARA FALLS)

A river takes a mighty leap and knocks
its tidy curls to ribbons on the rocks.
A cheap concrete city that's slapped on the edge
of the pit is inured to the maddening power.
A gardener trims a hedge
and dead-heads all the flowers.

Contempt and malice mingle in a stare,
and wrath foams up behind the tousled hair
that is made of the mist, and between the moist lips
there's a pleasure boat ferrying seers to the sight,
whose still shots of the trip
will come out flat and white.

A never-ending froth spills over.
Awe inspires the gawping tourists, with the roar
of the uncontained river regaling their ears.
The town is a tick in the mane of the mist,
as if the tacky years
of man did not exist.

Tim Ellis

QUESTIONS

Oh Spring born from out of the
death of last summer gone,
What is this phenomena redone?
Where organised, and where the goal?
What of the glory forming around
our very wonder of it all?

In your sweet nature our senses enthral,
So let us rejoice in your benevolence,
To man and beast and creatures all,
And we, what of ourselves and why born?
What will the death of our
last Summer spawn?

A cocoon of blue haze poison over all the land?
Choking our children, and theirs, our very own,
As they reach for oxygenizer and breath implore,
A rampant sun searing the heart
from out of our once beautiful land,
Will their last Summer ever live?
So Spring no more?

JR Richardson

UNTITLED

Pulsating, damaging thoughts are swimming.
Cluttered mind is over-brimming
brain's been re-wired and needs re-wiring
poisoned cells now, it's no good him crying.
Bad chemicals flow where the life-blood should go.
A deterioration of the healthiest mind
oh drug users can look forward to such a good time.

James Slater

TO TOWN

We went to town today
the four of us,
Sharon and I,
my unborn child
and the cancer in Sharon's belly.

We talked desultorally
of this and that, as friends do.
The baby shop magnetted me,
I must prepare for this new life within me,
must nest.

Then into garish supermarket
with endless music,
pierced by metallic loud-tannoyed voice
tintinnabulating in our ears.
We roved the trolley aisles
picking our needs
then to impersonal check-out.

Sharon drags wearily homewards
her embryo is taking its toll,
we part with smiles, stilted words,
I know her days are numbered,
what can I say - she knows too.

We went to town today
the four of us,
Sharon and I,
my unborn child
and the cancer in Sharon's belly.

Joan Wilson

GIVE MORE LOVE

The West sells weapons, civilians are attacked.
Street child earns a living hell by lying on her back.
Babies are born addicted to crack.
Give more love.

Money comes first, who cares about pollution?
Half the world is starving, we offer no solution.
To win votes they promise the earth, it is an illusion.
Give more love.

Love is stronger than the torture of war
As kidnapped families reunite.
Love for freedom stops Tiananmen tanks
And shatters the walls of apartheid.

Evangelist is busy saving defraud money.
So many people are homeless, so cold and hungry.
Racism of the human race shows our inhumanity.
Give more love.

Jeremy Scott

SUNDAY AFTERNOON

Gently blows the breeze
Bright shines the sun
Trees in green of every hue
Purple pansies, daisies white, cornflowers
of the deepest blue

Green and soft the grass
Butterflies flutter from flower to flower
Quiet broken only by the drone of a plane
birds singing
and the distant sound of traffic.

Here in the garden one is at peace
Wrapped round by the warmth of the sun
A sense of well-being pervades the mind
Beholden beauty enters the soul
For Creator God, your presence is here.

Shirley Ludlow

ONE EVENING IN SUMMER

Euphoria of life, one summer evening, through an open front door;
  waves gently heard lapping at the edge of the shore.
Shimmering sea lay tranquil, hushed, at peace; last rays of
  light reflected ripples of water, which never ceased.

Fluffy grey clouds floated silently by,
  fusion of red woven into the sky.
Foliage quivered, as dusk's soft whispering breeze,
  sang as a House Martin swooped down with ease.

Darkening of sky, dusk's hour soon was past,
  sea and sky merged, night descended so fast.
Shadows lengthened, day from view slipped away; jewels of
  light sparkled on the black velvet cloak round Ravenscar Bay.

Lynda Milnes

QUIET MOMENTS

Gazing through my window on this dull and rainy day
I see songbirds flying swiftly to and fro
Cows and horses in the fields
Finding shelter under trees
Before the storm should break
Flowers in the gardens closing petals silently
Bowing heads against the driving winds.
Smoke curling - swirling out of chimney pots on high
From fires in the houses giving off a friendly glow -
People huddled round in cosy comfort listening to the radio
Children with their noses pressed against the windowpane
Watching as the raindrops trickle down.
Soon it will be over - once more the sun will shine
Life now refreshed takes on a brighter glow.

Roslyn Carr

RETRIBUTION

Is there to be no more time for us?
Is there no consolation in despair?
Is there 'midst winter's erudite remorse
No touch of summer's gladness in the air?

If you call, can I through answering come?
Is there only retribution for our song?
Is there no refuge in remembrance?
Is there no place where you and I belong?

Rita E M Hunter

AS YOU THINK . . .

Overwhelmed by problems,
Lying sleepless in the dark hours,
You blame government, employer, family, recession.
Caught between a rock and a hard place,
How to change your circumstances?

You have the power within you.
You can if you think you can.
Unable to control events around you,
You may alter your thoughts.
You know flower seeds produce blooms,
Weeds breed more of the same.
That is the immutable law of life.
So good thoughts bring success and happiness,
Bad thoughts lead to suffering and misery.

Visualise a positive outcome.
Act upon the thought.
Maintain a straight line to your goal.
With undivided concentration.
Inevitably you will succeed.

The human spirit will achieve anything,
When directed in the right way.
You have the strength to overcome each obstacle,
If you simply change your thoughts.

Peter Hicks

AT THE PARTY AND AFTERWARDS

I have returned from abroad, but not for good.
My brother gives me a welcome back party;

When my friends use beautiful words
I bite the tips of my fingers until they bleed.
And then, as they continue to talk,
I suck away at the world that gathers,
imagining that my friends do not notice.
They are words that I recognise but do not use.
They are words that swell like a new form of sugar,
or the expectation of sugar. How my mouth turns over
in anticipation.

Ann tells my the story of a decision she had made.
I chew, and wonder
why today's topics rush through me and are answered
with the simplicity of internal decisions,
slotting themselves worldly; yes, no, no, no.
Dreamily I word responses, obscuring
the dictionaries springing from my fingers,
tingling founts behind my back.

The empty hangers chatter in the wardrobe;
it's the season again.
I make boxes and fill them with over-used words,
small ones, blue, vintage
ones for children.
Words on the street glow on cigarette ends,
out the safe slits of car windows, misread in eyes and misheard on lips
It's time to cherish, to steal again,
to breed, to leech myself pure.
Voices curl my tongue and are unfamiliar;
conversation melts and recrystallises.

My skin is transparent and replaces itself.

Angie Scarth

TIME

How slow the clock ticks now, how slow:
The measured tread of immeasurable time,
Counting the seconds, minutes, hours,
The days, the weeks, the months, the years,
And in the process spends the time
Which it would seek to count
And time, once spent, is past recall.
A moment is, and then is gone,
But still the hands move round the clock,
Devouring the time with greedy bites
And all the while, as we watch time,
Life slips by us, stealthily,
Until we note with startled gaze
That time, and life, for us, have flown.

Richard Young

YORKSHIRE

This timeless land of hill and dale
And carefree clouds in curdled skies,
Where lonely churches huddle away,
Eye-spied by curious passers-by.

Ruins stand with ancient pride,
Their memories scattered amongst each fallen stone,
Mansions beam in upheld splendour,
Tracing times worn by those now unknown.

Sheep-dotted fields run into valleys,
Moors stretch out on cushioned heather,
Windy seashores chase the oceans
While calling gulls circle round together.

This timeless land of hill and dale,
Beholden to none and welcoming to all,
Deserving only praise and honour,
Respect for Nature's beauteous call.

Jacqueline Fletcher -Hay

MAGIC LAND

Childhood is a precious time
It should be built on joy
Always keep the wonder of it all
For every girl and boy

In these times of push and rush
There is little time for play
But if I was the ruler of this world
I would have my say

I would turn the earth upside down
And make a childhood land
Just close your eyes and drift back in time
And then you'll understand

Go to sleep my little one
And dream the night away
Just take my hand to magic land
And another day

We'll fly through the sky on a marshmallow cloud
With wheels that are made of gold
With hats of silk and teddy bear coats
To stop us getting cold

We'll take a ride on a chocolate car
Along the Disney Road
We'll see a pig with silver wings
And a paper toad

All the people in this land
Is everyone you know
Like Rupert Bear and Donald Duck
And even Pinocchio

I'll take you to jelly wood
Where Smarties grow on trees
We'll have tea with Santa Claus
And feed the cola bees

We'll go to sea on a turnip boat
And fish for apple pie
And sail to Toy Town Land
With crisps up in the sky

And when we leave this magic land
The toys will wave goodbye
And on the back of a golden swan
To home we will fly

Then I will lay your head upon your bed
And kiss your fears away
For all that's nice will stay with you
And never fade away

I know you think I'm a dreamer
And this could never be
But if just one child was made happy
It would mean the world to me

Terry White

MICKEY THE GUIDE DOG PUPPY

The local paper advertised
For a possible volunteer,
To raise a guide dog puppy
To nurture and to rear.
Contacting the people in question
Having first consulted my spouse
I couldn't believe what they told me
That they'd come and inspect my house.

This person who came to inspect us
Said, 'I'm sorry but this won't do,
Places the pup is at risk from -
Really ought to be very few,
Those ranch doors into the kitchen
Must be changed, he needs a safe place,
If you put a proper door there,
Then the pup will have his own space.'

Would you believe when we got him
This loveable bundle of fun,
Right from the start 'til he left us
This pup had us both on the run.
The name they gave him was Mickey
Which suited him down to a T,
But that's not the name I called him
When he used my new rug for a wee.

The rules that we had to adhere to
We followed whatever our mood,
Blowing three blasts on a whistle
Meant Mickey could eat his food.
He learned about public transport,
With a trip on a bus and a train,
Exploring his environment,
Investigating new terrain.

The day came for him to leave us,
It was time for Mickey to go,
I knew how much we would miss him
Of course it was a wrench you know,
I cuddled him and I kissed him
With a mournful tear in my eye
Not a backward glance he gave me,
Farewell dear Mickey and goodbye.

Marlene Jackson

MY GARDEN

My garden is a source of joy to me,
For in its borders peace with beauty lies.
I know its every plant, each bush, each tree,
And every flower that buds and blooms and dies.
From worldly pressures here I can be free,
My spirit with the thrush and chaffinch flies.

Each season brings a beauty of its own.
A time to pause and watch, to sit and gaze
At Springtime daffodils by cool winds blown,
Or seek the shade in sultry Summer's haze.
In Winter when the swallows all have flown,
Then scarlet berries brighten gloom filled days.

In mid-September when the sky is blue,
And bedding plants are clothed in colours bright,
The grass is wet with early morning dew,
And dawn creeps late to banish chilly night,
Then fruit-hung trees are bathed in golden hue,
And shadows lengthen in the mellow light.

I love the painted lady's velvet wing,
And insects wakened by the sun's warm ray,
To hear the birds that from the tree tops sing
By quiet pools where dancing sunbeams play,
Where darkling toadstools spread their magic ring
Find tranquil stillness at the close of day.

Beryl Martinnant

PERFECTION

Softly, softly, take your time the day has nearly
ended and ultimately everything is fine.

So the pleasures have been gratifying for you
have taken part in the gifts God has created
which are miraculously extending.

Very soon it will be time for slumber because
quickly the sun, giver of life, will fade into
the west.

Now we have peace and quiet so don't forget
to say a little prayer and look to the east.

If you have accomplished all these things
with affection the end will be Perfection.

J White

VOID

Twelve-fifteen, and he's bang on time,
Expecting her ready to leave; prepared and packed
Like a parcel awaiting collection.
She's made up her mind; three nights in Wales
Is poor compensation for payment extracted -
Besides, she has an ache that will not
Go away of its own accord.

A stubborn molar, firmly packed and cruelly placed
Pierces the raw exposed softness of inner flesh -
Penetrating, distorting, infecting - there is
Nothing to be done save gouge it out.
But the operation is deferred -
For this week, he reminds her, he is hers;
'Time is precious,' and she is persuaded.

The quest for painkillers on her arrival
Finds Monmouth weeping in sympathy,
And she is soaked with tears from the sky -
To mingle later with her own
In the lonely comfortless room,
Where even the dog pees on the carpet
To show her disdain.

Only the child is excited, singing 'Inspector Gadget',
And the tune from the Coco-Pops advert -
Thinking this is his new home, asking;
'Where will we have breakfast, mummy?'
All is explained, but the child still sings
As 'the lovers' argue from separate beds -
The void between them unfilled, gaping.

Christina Clarke

PERI AND THE BLUEBIRD

Come in through
     the oak door,
Out of the blanket
     of snow,
Come in and I'll
     guide you
Through the trees,
Where golden apples
     grow in spring.
Where silver fountains
     play on flowers.
A garden for the
     young to stay;
A garden for the young -
     in heart
To pray.

Irene Patricia Kelly

AUTUMN

Cold and grey,
Yorkshire rain,
splashes on the window pane.

Leaden sky,
Autumn set,
dull and cold and drenching wet.

Distant hills,
Paradise,
turgid streams that rush and rise.

Backs of sheep
wet and cold,
soon transformed to watered gold.

Cold and grey,
Yorkshire rain,
splashes on the windowpane.

Joyce Harrington

UNREMEMBRANCE OF THINGS PAST

He could never
Remember whether
He had loved once or twice
Because of this
He felt cheated

When his body had
Finally persuaded him
That he was old
It did so
With the promise
Of past remembrance
Reliving old times
His great love affair
Of the centuries

But all he had
Was the uncertainty
Had it been one affair
With someone
Who'd dyed their hair
Or had he decided
At some juncture
That he preferred brunettes
Or did he marry the blonde
Misremembering Anita Loos

It's so frustrating
Spending your time
Trying to remember
What you have to remember

Ian Dannatt

CRAZY LOVERS

Crazy lovers,
Walking hand in hand.
Across the beach,
And warm white sand.

Crazy lovers,
Madly in love.
Thought they were,
Flying high above.

Crazy lovers,
Drifting apart.
Each taking with them,
A broken heart.

Emma Louise (15)

WHAT'S NEW?

Imagination - *omnivore*
Predation of the senses
A feeding frenzy on a good day
Autophagy in time of need
Appeasing creative hunger
By the scavenger's trawl
Of past lives and living thought

Reprocessing - the *prime* function
To deal in anagrams
Jumbling the seen and heard
Into wilful permutations
Wantonly rephrasing the past
Trading in obscure variations
On a theme of, 'All my own work'

Some hope - *still* hope
Of novelty
Utterance utterly new
Thought without precedent
Only present from the moment
t-zero
Unlinked to memories and reactions

Stephen H Hogg

FOR THINE IS THE KINGDOM

Is there Power beyond mankind,
A Power to change life's courses?
We need to plead, beseech and beg
To rally that Power's forces.

Something has to alter things,
Their sorrow - such a burden -
Humankind, we'll intervene,
But our aid cannot spare them.

We see them from the forest, saved,
Children, babies even -
Abandoned, lost, just left to fate -
Appeal to the Power, or be beaten.

A thread of life, a pulse still beats,
But the dying hearts are fading -
The hollow eyes, the vacant stares,
Despair - Death's so degrading!

Onto the train in desperation
Those who can move and breathe,
They scramble into carriages,
Too many - They're dying to leave.

Call on the Power beyond mankind,
We must rally in civilised prayer,
Beseech and plead with the unseen Great
And pray for the lives in Zaire.

Liz Rotheram

SOLITUDE

All by myself,
Just sitting here,
There's nobody anywhere near.
Solitude.

Peaceful and quiet,
I am at rest,
The world is at its best.
Solitude.

The shady trees
Sway in the gentle breeze,
While the sun beats down
On town.
Solitude.

A bird is singing
A merry tune,
While the grass is whisp'ring to the flowers in full bloom.
Solitude.

Mother's calling.
I make my way homeward,
Across the ford.
Goodbye, solitude.

Jane White (11)

HIDDEN SOUL

A hidden soul behind the eyes
Crying for the times gone by,
Of feelings lost
Of shadows cast
Of yearning for a youthful past.

A hidden soul that's not grown old,
Still trapped within the wrinkle fold.
And beauty born
Of nature's sorrow
Harkens for a bygone morrow.

A hidden soul that knew no bounds,
Love's danger gained
Love's anger found
And future days a distant dream,
Never to know what might have been.

E Garbutt

THE TIN FISHER
(A TRAMP)

He was Mr John Doe
Crawling the stinging summer streets of '81
As the radio promised an end to the despair of Wall Street's wail.
It meant nothing to him,
Except maybe more in his tin when the news filtered down.

The rain mustn't come yet he begged -
& he begged.

The Hare Krishnas got more notice than he,
Maybe it was time to change his religion -
Money is God, not good.

The drains made the subway a funnel -
He thin & going down:
The fuel
Of the city's progress.

There is no piety in his change.

At the bottom
Of his tin
He is a dragon,
A fable for children to learn:
Feared for being seen
Yet not existing anymore.

Gary T Pollard

MEMORIES

If I were to die tomorrow
what would become of yesterday?
All that joy and now the sorrow
where the pain won't go away.

What used to be a sandy beach
with sky-blue waves quite near.
Is now a sharp-stoned path
which seems to stay right here.

The whispers of the willow
weeping high and high.
No more a happy apple tree
blossoming by and by.

But out of the dust and the fog
I may see a light.
A light that's warm and peaceful
shining very bright.

So all these happy memories
I shall take with me.
Along my tiresome journey
memories, of the apple tree.

Amy McGarry (12)

THE END

Alone beneath the cruel sun he had to stand,
the last survivor of a noble band.

With selfless bravery his friends had fought so well -
but one by one before the enemy they fell

The ground baked hard, was hot beneath his feet.
But he must stand his ground despite the heat.

Surrounded by his foes who mocked his plight
yet he must show no fear, but stand and fight.

With sweat-dimmed eyes, he saw the charge begin
his fate bore down before him swift and grim.

The raised arm flashed, and he was rooted to the spot.

He heard the crack - and knew the bails were off.

Janet Cavill

IMMIGRANTS

With moistened eyes they left this rock
A weathered cracked and mossy tor,
Named it well 'departure point',
Then sailed to find another shore.

Did they find in lands afar,
The *El Dorado* of their dreams?
Did nagging home sickness drown,
The highest hopes of wealthy schemes?

Many folk crave for a change,
To flee from the daily grind,
When they've sped a thousand miles,
Their happiness was left behind.

Peter Rouse

MOM AND DAD

Parents are the ones
To love and cherish dearly
To me they do no wrong
We should treasure them surely
They comfort us when we are down
And give us love when we need it
Their love is all around
The most we should make of it
If there are times when we're feeling sad
Let's not sit around and mope
They're there to help, Mom and Dad
We'll all realise that one day I hope

Jacqueline Lill-Hirst

SILVER ODE

Music hath charm, as with poetry, prose.
With understanding, the joy these give grows
But of all the feelings 'neath heaven above
None can I cherish sublime as your love
Which desires and reflects my deep love of you
So patient and constant, so sincere and true.

Alan Fisher

RIGHTEOUSNESS

Wishful thinking opens the gates,
may my blood boil as I kill the intruder.
A great darkness filled my heart with envy, and I felt the coldness reach
the rosebuds.
But the petals did not perish among hell's flames,
they opened up their eyes to the fiery breath of freedom.
With hands of dirt they bathed in the light,
they rejoiced in the strife of the land.
Chains and burdens drowned in the tears of despair,
and the love in the world hugged them,
and gave them eternal rest in their souls.
The outside will once again join nature's call, and the darkness reigns
once more.
Love is waiting for people to decide, to make their decision,
and the enlightenment is waiting to be born.
Hope and death are waiting for their paths to be tread upon.
Let your dreams overcome your common sense,
and set the friendship free to carry its message.
Maybe one day we can hold each other's hands, and be united.
And for once the pathway may be clear, true justice may be done.
With no obstacles in our way, our hope can put aside persecution.
And then we can truly say with pride and dignity,
we are the united people.

Hannah Killala

BUTTERFLY

There is no savagery or ruthless vice
In this unchained flower,
Dragon-flamed wings ignited
By the snaking-grasses fuse.

Mantras of war are for birds, beasts and men
To chant incessantly
Until they draw
Their last rattling battle-breath:

You rise from the killing-grounds
To celebrate the sun,
A nectar-primed power-pack
Crackling with the potency of flight.

Flashing over a tree-bordered twilight of water,
Born with the weed-seed
On singing sedge-combed breezes
Which stir the haystack's flaxen thatch:

You are an aeolian ghost
Brought on a wind of dreams from lost childhood,
Red admiral of blushing skies
Haunting sorrel-smoked spinneys of summer:

Evoking from time-buried years
A laughing bright-eyed innocence, which drove
My agile body through swaying wheatfield dawns
Dense with the kindling colours of quivering wings.

I caught you clinging to a bending poppy's plume
Like a fragment of the setting sun,
Ephemeral as smoke, yet graceful in your dying,
Bowing out to the cloud-crinkled evening.

Dave Austin

HARMONY

Music is never so sweet
When everyone sings the same tune.
A breathless strain is best when like
Children
Some stop for breath at the beginning
Others at the end:
Some can't quite
Grasp it, and break off in the middle.
Some are a little off key,
Some sing their own
Unique
Melody

Gail Vernon

THE SAME SUN

It seems to have been forever
This nation torn apart by war,
Where those born into violence and crime
Must have wondered from time to time,
What all the bloodshed and hatred is for . . .

A war where families of soldiers
Are schooled in carrying the tricolour with pride,
A war fought on many different shores
To memories of a long-forgotten cause,
And apparently God is on both sides . . .

This world is an ever-constant battlefield
A global-wide legacy of grief,
Religion has a heavy price to pay
A reflection upon the gods to which we pray,
A side effect to the convictions of our beliefs . . .

So is anything ever solved
By the power of a bullet from a gun,
Whether Ireland or Vietnam
Africa or Afghanistan,
We all have to live under the same sun . . .

Keith Tissington

BEGINNINGS

The cave of my intimate dwelling, esoteric darkness,
cocoons, caresses.
An illusion of protection is not hopeless it swaddles,
swathes.

Separate yet connected, strands of tissue and blood,
holding, healing.
Creation to hold fast to the pulse if it could to
soothe, seal.

Aqueous surroundings perceive life, reaching, growing
into moving and meaning.
Never a moment like this uniqueness becoming,
naming, knowing.

Christl Kettle

BELONGING

I scan across the valley,
Early on this summer morn,
The horizon like a rooftop plateau,
The town where I was born.
But a stranger now,
Through needs of life,
Because it is that way,
I was a child within those rooftops,
'Twas where I first saw light of day.
You may settle far away,
Or around this world you'll roam,
But the place where you were born,
In your heart is always home.

Ken Lowe

WE ARE THE PEOPLE WE MAKE THE CHOICE

We are the people we make the choice
To speak on our own or have one voice
We are the Masters the Lords of the few
In days of old when time had a view

We did what we did just to escape
The cruelness of lust, pillage and rape,
Our Lords and Masters did things so dire
They threw poor souls upon the funeral pyre

The hideous masked ones the Lords of all
With bright helms and shields with which to enthral
They wreak such havoc they murder and brawl
Where is our hero, where is our Lord?
Should we put our faith in God?

Then the darkness comes to us all over again
No Radio Four or Big Ben
Just a whisper in the dark night
Where have all the brave men gone?
Which Saviour will rise to take us home?

Eddie Sykes

JULIE'S HEART

A nebulous seduction to some moon-drenched misty shore
Dare I walk on in, step right through the monster's jaws?
This a place of stolen pleasure taste forbidden fruits
Colours melding always changing earth it shifts beneath my boots
Plane of whispers dancing shadows can't remain here for too long
Real event or fevered dream a long-forgotten childhood song

Your forests so enchanted yield their memories to me
Altered textures light unknown not quite sure of what I see
Tiny movement send my eyes to where the secret seems to play
Leave too soon but if I could I'm not sure whether I would stay
Bitterness as well as sweet both dark and light in this terrain
Beauty tasted but beneath is subtle sting, the flavour pain

A citadel of leaf and vine and crystal voices in my ears
Perhaps the last remains of Eden, I guess the serpent still feeds here
And roses bloom in emptiness like twilight's last lament
But you were longer in the desert, come back home my sweet nepenthe
The mystery mine for a second in time, a fragment of infinity
A silver tear to kiss our souls then crystallize eternally

Ian Sen

OUR CHOSEN CHILD

We had no children of our own, although we tried our best.
Sought doctor's help, took all advice, and each and every test,
Adoption, then, was our next plan, 'You'll have to wait,' they said,
And wait we did, and time went by, our goal seemed years ahead.

The days, the weeks, the months passed on,
And soon another year had gone,
We hoped and prayed, and longed and yearned
Until, at last! Good news we learned.

Our chosen child, our son and heir,
With eyes of blue and hair so fair,
This child to fill our hearts with love,
Seemed heaven-sent from God above.

He fills our home with love and light,
Our hearts with joy from morn till night.
So round, so sweet, so fair of face,
No other child could take his place.

And now he carries on the line,
The future's bright, the outlook's fine,
With doting Grans and Grandads, too,
Dear Son, we think the world of you.

Connie Hird

IT'S YOU

It's you, it's you
Yes you.
Who wakens with
The morn.

It's you, yes you.
Who knows what
Faces you today.

It's you, yes you.
Who can take
The strain.

It's you, yes you.
Not physician's aid
Nor surgeon's skill,
Can make the day.

It's you, yes you.
Who has to
Carry on,
No matter what
Has gone.

It's you, yes you,
Who faces life
Unknown.

It's you, yes you,
Who has to make
It all worthwhile.

Jack Allerston

BIRTHDAY MEMORIES

(For Jean Whitfield, Stoke-on-Trent, April 15 1995)

Today is your birthday dear Mother
We know you will understand
Why we cannot speak birthday greetings
Nor touch with ours, your dear hand.
No birthday kiss can we give you
Nor hand you a floral bouquet
But hearts that will always remember
Are thinking of you fondly today.
Time with its tears will move slowly
But memories will never grow old
Because the strong bonds of love that bind us
Are dearer than silver or gold.

Mary Ferguson

ADOLF HITLER'S HANDS

Down beneath the whirlpool,
Underneath the sea,
Down where the ocean's darkness is alive,
Or seems to be,
Under the water,
Very near the sands,
Waiting there expectantly
Are Adolf Hitler's hands.

Down beneath the whirlpool,
Near to the shore,
Adolf Hitler's hands embrace
The world and look for more,
In the dark cave
Near the whirlpool in the bay,
Adolf Hitler's grasp is stronger
Than I care to say.

Underneath the ocean,
Down in the caves,
Adolf Hitler's hands are moving
Underneath the waves.

Peter Wade

FROM HERE

He'll have words,
But they won't be
Specific or tried.
He'll take steps,
But they won't be
Too long in the stride.
He'll take arms,
But he'll always
Be neutral inside.
If the weather is fair
He'll be there.

John Holgate

PORTRAIT

You laugh inexplicable mystery:
It must feel strong to be
So alone. A tweak of your cap
Or vicious laugh splinters a lesser mortal.
My Bosela, unbelieving priest.
You torture to seek weakness
And gain no reassurance.
You laugh irreplaceable mystery
And dream irresponsible logic.

Louise Wade

MENTAL EXILE

She wears a face with no expressions
A mind without fear
With eyes full of happiness
Yet so full of tears
She has no consolations
No shoulder to cry on
She lets bygones be bygones
Because there's no-one to rely on
Her expressions are hidden in a veil of confusion
Her mind is a vortex filled with paths of illusion
An empty void where there once was quality
Now an escape from the world
A retreat from reality
Her mind's been disturbed
Her life has been pillaged
Now she is all alone in her altered image.

C J Collins-Reed

RIVER BARGES

Three bridges stride the river
Dividing city east from west
Water brown and murky as
A fleet of barges pass
Steering down the narrow channel
Every day a hazardous task.

Drypool, Myton whichever route is taken
The traffic queues along the street
Waiting for a bygone age of barges
Cobbled lanes and plodding feet
The flour mills stand sentinel
Where rivers Hull and Humber meet.

The bargeman smiles as he passes
And waves to the traffic up high
His life is slow and peaceful
In tune with the seagulls and sky
As he heads for the open water
Where foreign cargoes lie.

Rita Fisher

TRAVELLING DAYS

There is a place from my childhood days
That added brightness in thousands of ways
Airport lounges where we had our long waits
Coach terminals with barriers, shut behind gates
Railway stations with bare waiting rooms
Us kids running riot, porters fume.

Still, as a child it never worried me
Travelling was fun, plenty to see
Relatives to wave us off and cry
Me and the others waving goodbye
Often we didn't know for where we were bound
Tucked up in flight, we slept sound.

Joy and pleasure at our journey's end
Reunited with parents on whom we depend
Happy to be back as one again
Forgetting the tears, parting and pain
Once more a new life to start
Feelings of happiness showered my heart.

Connie Moss

OUT OF CONFUSION

How are we to know
The right way to go?
Who do we trust?
How do we know?
We've got to try. We must
Otherwise we end up poor
Poor in spirit lacking trust.

Who do we ask?
What do we do?
Do we lack faith?
Ho, do it yourself.
Some might say,
'Make and effort,
Think it through.'

My God
I put my trust in you
I have that trust and faith
Enough to start anew
And take this positive step
The one that certainly
Rings true.

Dan Brown

KERKIRA

Enchanted island. . . the Scheria of Homer,
Weaving its own special kind of magic on you,
The air sweetly scented with lemon and orange;
Grove upon grove, stretching endlessly, come in to view.
Golden sandy beaches sloping very gently
Into the sea . . . pretty isle so richly glowing,
Vibrant with blossom and broom, blazing with colour,
And the grey-ashy green of olive groves growing,
Gnarled and misshapen, broken by clustered Cypress
Trees, tall symbols of mourning, in their dark green dress.

Follow down the dusty road, lazily winding
Through sylvan landscape and there, well-spotted, is Pan,
Playing his pipes, mischievous god gaily prancing
Along with nymphs and naiads looking palely wan.
The light subtly changes and the spirits of wood
And water are goats and sheep, stood tethered to trees
At the roadside, warily watching passers-by
With slitted eyes brimming with mischief, nibbling leaves.
And donkeys, with bundles of hay, are meekly led
By dark-clothed girls, carrying water on their heads.

Gwendoline Douglas

LAIRGATE, BEVERLEY, EAST YORKSHIRE

It was an April day
when I walked that way
to register the death of a loved one.
Administrative niceties softened
the dull realisation that the last 'goodbye' is for ever.
'A blessing', 'he was ready' - platitudes well-meant,
but not disguising that, unknown to me, I was not.

The street was the same as ever - plain or elegant:
as it had been a thousand times over forty summers
as I had hurried on inconsequential errands,
never really forming a firm impression of it.
It would now always remind me of this.

No more 'next week we will's', no more birthdays,
the Christmas rituals, diluted by time; improved even,
now transformed for ever.

The passers-by go about their business, it is not their turn.
The old street echoes, perhaps winks as the sun flits across glass -
will it know that
it was an April day
when I walked that way,
and changed how I saw it for ever?

Christopher Gale

THE ACTORS

From centre stage
Wearing garb befitting their roles
With lighting, and props, positioned expertly
The actors took the writer's imagination
Turning it into reality
Into the captive audience's open minds
They played to the end relentlessly
Amid thundering applause
They took their bows
And left the stage triumphantly.

J M Harman

AFTER THE RAIN

It's a beautiful morning, after the rain
as the watery sun starts to shine.
It's a morning of glory as little birds sing
and it feels like the whole world's got time.
But the news on the TV's depressing
all the hurt and the heartache and pain,
so I give thanks for this beautiful morning
after the night and the rain.

Audrey Woodall

LAST WISHES

Show me Heaven!
Show me Hell!
Give me strength, and make me well,
Show me power,
I'll show you pain,
Show me all the things
I'll not see again.
Show me money,
I'll show you greed.
Show me a car, and show me speed.
Take me out in the morning sun,
Let me see others
Having such fun.
Show me the places I've never been.
Loan me a video I've never seen.
Visit me often and don't be shy,
Pray for me often,
Just till I die.

Arthur Lammiman

SWEET ENCOUNTER

It was a day in June, like most of the rest,
The work and the play, the jokes and the jest,
When all of a sudden, quite out of the blue,
As *I* was out walking, my eyes fell on *you*.
I knew at that moment my life was mapped out,
This was the day I'd been dreaming about,
All I'd believed in and acted upon
Was coming to me, my problems all gone.
A rosier future was *my* lucky lot,
Your style and your grace, and those eyes made me hot,
The cut of the suit and the shoes polished bright
Were all to my taste, and the height was just right.
I knew from the first you were looking at *me*
And heading my way, *my* feelings to see.
My legs turned to jelly as you took hold of my hand
And you asked me, so quietly, 'What is your brand?
Would you please help? It's a survey you see.
Do you use sugar, or put *these* in your tea?'

Greta Leadbeater

To Lose The One You Love

To lose the one you love
How sad it makes you feel inside
You're lost and lonely
To know the one you love has died.

You'll miss their kisses
And their loving tenderness
You'll miss their arms around you
And their warm sweet caress.

So to lose the one you love
When it makes you feel lost inside
Is to think of all the good times
Then the tears will flow less as you cry.

Mary Shaw-Taylor

SPORTING TREES

The poplar trees stand tall and proud,
Like sentinels above the crowd
Who gather round the village green,
To watch their local cricket team.

The strong and sturdy forest oak,
Does wear its foliage like a cloak,
Which makes it difficult to see
The golf ball's wild trajectory.

The willows dip their weeping fronds
In ripples set with diamonds,
As past them glide with flashing oars
The huffing puffing coxless fours.

The aromatic mountain pines
Cast shadows over wavy lines,
As hurtling on their winding way
Exhilarated skiers sway.

The city planes breathe tainted air,
And struggle in the atmosphere,
Great gulps of which one needs to run
The yearly London Marathon.

The Avenue Des Champs Elysess's
Lined with Paree's finest trees,
As through without a backward glance
Speed riders in the Tour de France.

These varied trees bear witness to
The courage shown by all of you,
Who challenged by a sporting dream
Beat all the odds, and reign supreme.

Jill Layden

A NEW TEMPLE

Life upon Mars
Red versus green
Life upon Earth
Too, we barely wean.

Cries of the destitute and hungry
Fall upon deaf ears
Rather keep the rockets soaring free
Progress without fears.

Earth soon a barren desert
Though the poor have watered it with tears
Advancement for future years
Wasting billions shooting for the stars
Many more deserts on Mars!

Of mice and men, perhaps we should choose the mouse
Even rodents don't defile their father's house.

Michael A Kelly

THE CIRCUS COMES TO TOWN

Bang, bang, beats the drum, can you hear it?
Bang, bang, beats the big bass drum,
The rest of the band and majorettes follow,
Announcing the circus has come.

People stare at the wagons trundling by,
Children shriek with laughter and joy,
For the circus had finally come to our town
Bringing happiness for each girl and boy.

In a field behind the Red Lion Inn
Passers-by watch as the big top is unfurled,
A man shouts, 'Come and see us tonight,
Come and see the finest acts in the world.'

On opening night the seats are all full,
In the ring sawdust covers the ground,
Fine horses and riders in their plumage
Start the show as they lightly prance around.

The clowns in their big baggy trousers
With garish paint daubed all over their face,
How the children laugh and giggle at them
As they throw water and foam round the place.

We see the fearsome lions and tigers,
Then huge elephants circle around,
We gasp in fear when trapeze artists appear,
One mistake, they would fall to the ground.

Now it is time for the circus to leave,
They are packed up all ready to go,
Maybe next year we shall see them back here
When the drumbeat heralds the show.

Barbara Sowden

BEFORE EASTER

It was the springtime of the year,
And the summer of his life,
When they came to crucify
Our Lord God, Jesus Christ.

The trees were out in bud,
And the birds were nesting by,
When our dear Lord, Jesus Christ,
Said his last goodbye.

They stripped him and they whipped him,
Then they lead him out of town,
Outside the city walls they took him,
And with thorns they made a crown.

They nailed him to a wooden cross,
Placed high above the ground,
He cried, 'Father forgive them,'
Then died without a sound.

Jean Ruth

CENTRAL RESERVATION

Serpent-like the tarmac gleams
In the new fallen rain.
Metal rolls along on rubber
Belching smoke and steam.
Where the grass grows long in the centre
Hemmed in by crash barriers, nature takes its course.
Bees sip nectar from clover clumps
Flies hover over an animal corpse
And a pair of birds begin a nest.

In a young green sapling,
Unconcerned by noise and chaos,
Road rage, horns honking,
Speed merchants and squealing tyres . . .
The two birds begin to feed in answer
To the four gaping beaks in shrill cry.
A constant stream of caterpillars
Passes through their beaks.
Young wings grow stronger, beating the air.

In amidst the mechanical mania,
As police remove wreckage,
They finally take to flight,
Leaving the green strip oasis behind
For an urban garden where old age
Prevents speed and change
And nature thrives unchallenged by man.

Sandra Fisher

I Wonder

As beneath the sky I sit
And wonder how it all began,
The sun, the moon and all the stars
Who put them there and why?

Who dressed the trees in leafy green?
Who gave the birds their song?
The snow, the rain, the dew, the mist,
Who did all this and why?

Who gave the winds their icy breath?
Who gave the warmth to shield?
The flowers, fruit and berries bright,
Who did all this and why?

As beneath the sky I sit,
And wonder how it all began,
I ask not why, and wonder,
I just give thanks to God.

Sheila McMillan

HOMELESS

As I walk through the streets
With nowhere to stay
I'm wondering aimlessly
Living day by day.

For some life is easy
For others oh so hard
What will they sleep on tonight
Me? Well, mine's a bed of card.

I have no-one to care for
No-one cares for me.
Sat alone with an empty bottle
Thinking is this how life should be.

I look at my clothes, tattered and torn
They do their job - that's to keep me warm
Unshaven face, hair full of grease
Just food and a whisky
I'll die in peace.

John Broadbent

FIXATED

The night you left, I did not see,
The next day you were gone.
You took away a part of me,
From two in love to one.

Yet still I tried to feel no pain,
I thought I could be strong.
I'm used to living on my own
But now it just seems wrong.

So now I live another day
Determined not to crack,
But somehow you fixated me
And now I need you back.

Craig Porteous

THE WISHING DREAM (SUMMER IN HARDCASTLE CRAGS)

Before the sun had died away
To leave a scene of darkened day,
I sat upon a mossy stone
To watch the Autumn scene alone.
The valley lay so still below,
Where only darkened shadows grow,
The stirrings of the rocky stream
Lulled me into a wishing dream
Of a longing for past Summers' glory,
To write warm verse - a happy story.

The Autumn breeze though, broke the spell,
And another story I must tell,
Of a myriad of naked trees
That stiffly wave in the Autumn breeze.
They no longer house the lovelorn bird,
Nor their chatter overheard,
The acorn cup hangs empty now
Upon its gnarled gaunt bough.
The Summer leaves lie in withered grief,
Stolen by the Autumn thief.

I told the Autumn breeze to go,
To turn my mind from its sorrow,
I saw the trout rise from the stream
To snap a fly in a warm sunbeam,
Flower clusters smile along the bank,
Whose sweet nectar the insects drank,
Each morn I heard the Summer chorus
Of lovelorn birds in their leafy terrace,
This wishing dream my heart does yearn,
Oh, Summer! Quickly, to me return.

Cathy Pighills-Feather

FRUSTRATION

I hurried home in quite a fuss,
some news I had we must discuss,
I'd wait until we finished tea,
and get his whole attention, see?

I cleared away, chatting gaily,
although his eyes raked the daily,
then later on I had a peep,
oh now he's going off to sleep.

When he awakes, I'll give my news,
interesting will be his views,
you've guessed, there was another hitch,
he woke all right and turned the switch.

His eyes took in a cricket match,
I should have known there'd be a catch.
'What do you think?' I tried to say,
but clearly he was miles away.

He'd quite forgotten I was there,
it really was too much to bear.
Patience had reached desperation,
bursting with my information.

I racked my brain to find a scheme,
to get him on the gossip theme.
The public box, it's quite near home,
I'll tell him on the telephone.

Ivy Wood

ANCIENT AND MODERN

I saw the priest's embroidered cloak,
His jewelled staff and crucifix,
The silver senser, fragrant smoke,
And golden glittering candlesticks.
Golden his cape, golden his ring,
Golden the altar's precious plate,
The Bishop, splendid as a king
Was, like a king, enthroned in state.
Inside the church the sunshine bright
Through lofty stained glass windows sprayed
Patterns of iridescent light
Upon the righteous as they prayed.
Out of his seat their shepherd rose,
A shining figure tall and grave,
And soon his educated prose
Echoed along the vaulted nave.
What open heart could not be stirred
By such a scene in such a place,
And yet my straying thoughts preferred
To journey back through time and space.
Another face a distant land,
A crowded sunbaked mountain slope.
A gentle voice, an outstretched hand,
Words of wisdom, love, and hope.
No ornate finery I found,
No pomp, no pageantry - instead -
He climbed upon a dusty mound,
And, 'Blessed are the meek,' He said.

He died, they say, to save us all.
His name is often on our tongues.
The sad truth is that we recall
Only the singer, not the songs.

Jack Macfarlane

THE SAVERS OR KEEP IT IN THE FAMILY

Like my Grandmother before me
I save everything I can
'Just in case it may come in handy one day'
At least, that's what Gran used to say.

She used to save old clothes.
Bits of jewellery, buttons, and all that.
And for almost any occasion
She could always find you a hat.

I tend to be a bit of a hoarder.
There's buttons and pins, needles and things
All pushed untidily in the top drawer.
Most of them have no possible use to me any more.

So why go on saving them? You ask
I don't know why. I really can't say.
Perhaps I'm too idle to clean out the drawer,
I can't bear to throw things away.

My Grand-daughter is just the same.
Her bedroom shelves are crammed to the ceiling with books.
If you dare say, 'Take them all to a jumble sale.'
You may get some very funny looks.

She likes teddy bears too.
Paddingtons, Ruperts, Forever Friends,
Winnie the Poohs, to name but a few.
The list goes on, it never ends.

My husband, ex-joiner, handy man, King of his Trade
Has his drawers jammed with screws and hammers
Even the odd nail.
Bits of scruffy paper with drawings and dimensions on
For wonderful creations that simply cannot fail.

So it goes on the saving craze.
Sometimes it's not so funny
To fill your drawers with lots of nothing
When you ought to fill them with pots of money.

Betty Walton

ALONE

Alone she stood at the window
frail white hair and old.
Alone she stood at the window
looking out at the winter's cold.
Once she had a husband, children she had four,
gone now is her husband, her children are no more.
Sometimes she remembers winters of the past
when she and George and the children thought that things would last.
Happy days were many, though life was hard and grim
but family life was lovely, as she remembered them.
Children don't stay children, adults they become
their lives are full and busy, they've forgotten their old mum.
Alone she stood at the window, wondering where? When? Why?
as she looked at the line of photographs
of youth in days gone by.
Pause in your daily habits, stop and remember mum
who stands alone at the window
wishing for someone to come.

Elizabeth Crabtree

SEASONS

The babe is born
'Tis a happy morn
New parents proud
Joy's heard aloud.

The child he grows
To school he goes
Best years of life
All fun - no strife.

To youth from child
Drive's parents wild
Where lies the fault
Too late to halt.

A young man now
Knows why and how
Life of his own
His seeds are sown.

So age creeps on
Some friends are gone
Dad now grand-dad
Life's slow and sad.

An old man dies
But mid the sighs
Not all forlorn -
A grandson's born.

Tony Emmott

LOVE EVOLVES

My soul, it soared to Heaven
Through the starlit skies;
I even caught a glimpse of God
Through my newly-opened eyes.

As I amble through lush forests;
Laze in wondrous fields of dew,
Thoughts of love and tenderness
All converge on you.

Iridescent in beauty
You capture the light;
A glow like the moon's
Only visible at night.

Delightful, passionate - delicious;
Playful in your freedom
Gracefully you danced into my life;
To begin our time in Eden.

Fly now, my heart afire
Majestic like a dove
This one, goes out tonight
To the one I love.

David Sprosson

DAD'S BAD HABIT

We are thinking of ringing Childline,
My sister and I are being abused,
Abused might be a bit too strong,
More like we are being ill-used.

You see our Dad has really changed,
Changed into a right old grumps,
He used to be happy, full of fun,
Now he's always down in the dumps.

When he comes home from work now,
He shouts at the dog and the cats,
Where before he would gently stroke
And fuss, give the dog friendly pats.

When we have all eaten our evening meal
And the night's paper he has read,
He snaps, 'Have you two finished your homework yet?
If so, then be off to bed.'

Nothing now is right for him,
He's always picking on my sister and me,
All the programmes on the television he says
Rubbish, not worth the license fee.

He's not a jolly person any more,
Mum says for his sanity she is starting to fear,
He's not even happy at weekends now
After being out with his pals for a beer.

Mum has just told Dad in no uncertain terms,
About his behaviour we have cause to complain,
And we all know it's expensive and bad for his health,
But will he please start smoking again.

Frederick Sowden

GONE BUT NOT FORGOTTEN

Why did you have to do it?
Were you in so much pain
I feel a sadness for your loss
You had nothing to gain.

Why did you have to do it?
The time for you to go
Was not called by God above
And you leave behind the ones you love.

Why did you have to do it?
We didn't know you were that sad
You braved a smile for those around
But inner peace you could not find.

Why did you have to do it?
You leave behind your family
Who loved you very much
But tragedy comes when no-one sees,
And then a body lay still amongst the breeze.

Rosanna Ledwold

JEALOUSY

You always were the pretty one,
You always were the best,
You stood out incredibly,
While I intermingled with the rest.

You always had the perfect hair,
And a perfect smile,
And if you were to say 'jump'
Every lad would jump a mile.

I hated you with a passion,
Yet I loved you with all my heart,
I'd do anything you wanted,
Yet regretted knowing you from the start.

You were my best friend,
And we were as close as two friends could be,
The only thing that came between us,
Was that one thing jealousy.

Gemma Abrahams (16)

FEELING BLUE

When you're feeling down
When you're feeling blue
Pick up this little message
That I have sent to you.
You are a worthwhile person
So hold your head up high,
Keep the smile upon your face
And kiss those tears goodbye.
Take a real deep breath
Blow away your stress
Confidence appears to tackle all the mess.
Doesn't that feel great?
Tension will subside
Making you feel happy and glowing
With such pride
Simple are the steps
It's all you have to do
To disperse that negative energy
Which makes you feel so blue.

Michelle Quinn

LOVING GIFT

You came into my life at just the right time,
'twas going nowhere, had no reason or rhyme,
Giving me love, value and worth.
Turning frowns into laughter,
For you had great sense of mirth.

Your love of fine music tuned my deaf ear,
Your heart was the hankie that kissed away tear.
We always stood tall, our love like a wall,
No one could hurt us, no one at all.

You elevated my spirit to a plain on high,
This rare love we shared will never die.
When time comes to rest and dust we become,
May God in his goodness join our souls into one.

You came into my life at just the right time,
Thank you for giving it reason and rhyme.

M Rothera

The Way

Lord,
Show me the way I can somehow repay
The blessings you've given to me.

Lord,
Teach me to do what you want me to
Do and to be what you want me to be.

I'm unworthy I know
But I do love you so
I beg you, please answer my plea.

I've not much to give
But as long as I live
May I give it completely to thee.

James Manley

THE GARDEN

As daylight fades and shadows lengthen
The garden radiates amber and gold,
As if, in that fleeting moment,
Lifeblood flows from one to the other
In symbiotic harmony.
And in that perfect stillness
The balance of Nature is preserved.
Earth and sky
United in oneness
Reflected and reflecting,
Each drawing strength from the other
As the elements merge
To create a shining light,
Which penetrates the universe.

Linda Holbrook

EVENING

The eventide is slowly creeping in,
Comfortably, we watch from within.
A lost bird, is flying to roost,
We turn on the radio,
Our confidence to boost!

Quietness is descending all around,
Flowers close and bow their heads,
Children tired, yawning, ready for bed.

Slowly darkness is engulfing the Earth,
Dark clouds, heavy with rain,
Floating almost nimbly but low again!

Suddenly we find a break in the cloud!
Maybe, we can soon see a star.
Even the moon, to shine from afar!

To give light to the end of this day,
And help to guide us, on our way.
To lay our tired bodies to rest,
The only way, we know best.

Eva Rose

JULY MOMENT

Early morning, garden green,
Sweet peas and roses glowing, fragrant.
Air fresh, unbreathed, clean.

Soft, far-off engines - playing
On the Sunday motorway,
Aping busy buzzers.
No Sabbath for the bee
As it flies around me.

Bright, piercing sunlight
Igniting blobs of dew -
Encapsulated rainbows!

Sam, the cat, suddenly revealed,
Deeply snuggled beneath a bush;
Cattishly indolent, no rush.

'Hush,' I think, clipping away
At the spent glory of the senecio;
Bright yellow to grey.

Snip, snip. Sh, sh!. . .
See! I work - like the bee,
And summer slips along the way.

Marjorie Tetlow

UPLAND SIEGE

Cast square on ill-tholed ground
  Derelict and lying fallow Course crafted
In vulgar tones with shuffled bricks of wind
Raked stone Broke with tattered hackles
Framed in dusty sightless glass. All
Ungainly settled neath a sagging hat.

A blot in endless seething green set
Staunch against the glaring tussocks waiting
For snug life to stir mute air kindle
Blind eyes and set a beating heart
Within to fight the marching grass and quench
Its silent rage.

C F Horsfall

HOMELESS

He sat on the precinct, looking sad and forlorn.
The clothes that he wore were tattered and torn.
On an old woolly jumper, sat Tinker his dog,
Next to a hold-all, with a note pinned on, saying

He was blind, had no home or a bed,
He didn't have a job, or money it said.
Could you spare a few pence so I may eat,
And buy old Tinker a can of dog meat?

Crowds thronged by, this way and that,
Some threw money into his hat.
Tinker sat there as good as gold,
Guarding his master, like he'd been told.

Was he blind? Some were heard to say.
Is he a scrounger, who should be sent on his way?
Is he one who will beg and steal?
Or is he genuine and in need of a meal?

Once a proud soldier, his comrades all dead,
His war ended, with the wound to his head.
He remembered no past, family or wife,
He worked on the land, led a nomadic life.

Now he was ill, had pains in his head.
He came to the town, to find a room and a bed.
Time and again, he was turned away.
No one would have him and Tinker to stay.

Come tomorrow, he'd go to the church on the hill,
Sit on the steps and wait.
For God would come, open his door wide,
Invite him and Tinker to step inside
Into his heavenly home.

Rita Cocker

Rain

Today, it rained,
Large drops,
Drum, drum, drumming,
On the dustbin lid,
Splattering, splodging, spattering,
Running down,
Making little trickles,
Into puddles,
Rain.

The windowpane was hit,
With sharp needles,
Or witches pointed,
Fingernails, tapping and rapping,
Trying to,
Come in, to make us wet,
Make things drip,
With rain.

Dropping on seeds,
Tap, tap,
Wake up, time to,
Rise, bloom and look nice,
Poppies, buttercups, daisies,
Coming up,
Hoping for the sunshine,
After rain.

Soaking the cats,
Spit spat,
Spiking their fur,
Making them angry,
Spit cat, spit rain,

Soggy moggy,
Scratching on the window,
Waiting to come in,
From rain.

K Scatchard

As I Am

See me as I am
Take me by the hand
Tell me there's a way
Tell me that
You want me to stay
Look into my eyes
It's easy if you try
Comes as no surprise
You're the only one
That can make me cry.

When I'm on my own
My thoughts are all of you
I cannot help but think
Of all the things
You say and do
Now that time has passed
We've spent some time apart
You'll come running back
We can make a brand new start.

I'm not myself
When you're away
Instead of getting easier
It's getting harder every day
I'm hoping soon that you'll come home
I can't face it any longer
This feeling so alone.

You don't know me
As I am.

Russell Petcher

CATHEDRAL EVENSONG

Pure sound like light through stained glass
Harmonises with dappled water colours
Insubstantially resting on cathedral floor,
Sunshine through coloured panes
Set in tracery:
Then arches and blends with soaring curves,
Spanning the height of honeyed stone;
Cascades upwards like a spring,
Downwards like a sunlit fountain
Of streaming, myriad, liquid prisms,
Drawing me like a water diviner
To the moment, place where
The Divine crosses my soul's path
And I sense the still waters
Of the wells of paradise and
My soul doth magnify the Lord.

The Spirit's powerful gentleness
    alights,
        electrifies,
            sparkles,
                inspires,
                    glows.
And my spirit hath rejoiced in God my Saviour.

(To Ian Tracey and Ian Wells of Liverpool Cathedral whose names are included in the lines. Quotations from the Magnificat (Evensong).)

Christine Pallant

Our Pennine Village Year

Spring
Mallards are nesting by the river,
Daffodils in profusion adorn the churchyard,
Lambs gambol in the adjoining field,
And in the uncertain sunshine
I watched a blue-tit preen.

Summer
Silently among the sibilant reeds the heron stood,
We observed beside full foliaged trees on river bank,
Picnicking in shade, blue skies, bright warm sun, and smells of
  countryside,
The music of flowing river, hay-making in progress,
Long school holidays, sound of cricket ball hitting bat,
And strawberries and cream for tea.

Autumn
Purple heather on moors and hills,
Red, yellow and gold the leaves have turned,
Barns full, the harvest gathered in,
Festivals of thanks and praise in churches
To Him for His bounteous goodness and mercy.

Winter
Our homes prepared for winter gales and snow,
Wild bird seed and peanuts ready for our garden friends,
Padded jackets, scarves and gloves, and joyful yells of children
  sledging.
Church bells heralding the Holy Babe is born on Christmas morn,
And as the old year slips away, we welcome the dawn of New Year's
  Day.

E M Pucknell

ROZINA

With sad pale face
And tear-filled eyes
She rocks in her cot all day
And how I long to pick her up
And take her far away
From this cold damp institution
With its rows of rusting beds
Filled with unwanted babies
And unwashed children
With shaven heads.

For I have a home
Where she'd be loved
And given every care
But stony-faced officials
Say Rozina must stay there.

Oh, where's the justice?
Where's the sense?
Of these bureaucrats
With their official files
And don't speak to me
Of ethnic roots
For a little girl
Who's never smiled.

Marlene Hope

IRELAND

In the town of Ballymurphy
Two men walked along the street
A noise was heard, shots were fired,
The pavement slipped beneath their feet.
Someone, somewhere had been waiting
With hate in their hearts that day.
Was it the British soldiers or was it the IRA?
Confrontation to the coward, it isn't really on.
He hides away a mask on his face, trigger finger on his gun,
Will we ever know the reason, the wherefore or the why?
But in a divided country it is easy for men to die.

Margaret Cottam

HERO

Not too keen on swimming
He described his heroics
As being in the wrong place
At the wrong time.
And never one to talk a lot
We had to accept his version.

A short while later, the truth out,
He had been far braver
Than credit was given for,
Leaping into rushing waters
To save the life
Of some ungrateful stranger.

Risking life and limb
Not being part of his everyday routine
He wished it all forgotten,
But then, only days later
They fished her out again,
And this time she'd succeeded.

Tony Jones

PLOTINUS
(Greek Philosopher 205-270 AD)

In pain
the wise man
makes a decision
to accept

He retains his freedom
raises the level of his nature
sets at naught
all else
that terrifies the mind

Not pain,
touching the sage
as it touches the common man,
nor sorrow
piercing his inner soul
gain him to cry out
before
the miseries come

In pain
ask no pity,
for the inner soul
has a radiance
untroubled by suffering
as a candle within a lantern
is sheltered
from the storm

pain
said the sage
is an arena
where the powerful combatant
holds his ground.
Cease then, to complain
at what pain
might be.

Una Stothard Smith

THE DAFFODIL

How beautiful the daffodil,
So undeterred by winter's chill.
A sign that spring is on the way,
And warmer weather here to stay.

Each golden head is held up high
Each bud is pointing to the sky,
They open more with each new day,
As sunshine warms with gently ray.

They stand so proud, their colours bright,
A mix of yellow, orange, white,
So cheerful after winter's gone
With other blooms to follow on.

But as the seasons come and go,
And other flowers start to grow
And gardens bare with colour fill
My favourite's still the daffodil!

Sheila Gannon

HOPE

Hope is deep
It never fails
To reawaken
The farthest dream
To walk with hope
Leaves sadness alone
To live with hope
Fulfils the dream.

Caroline Davis

Autumn Tapestry

Brisk bright autumn morning,
Autumn leaves so gently falling.
The playful frisky wind is nigh
Racing the leaves as it goes by.

The smell of woodsmoke in the air,
What memories in that scent there are.
A rustling leaf carpet beneath my feet,
These are the joys of autumn sweet.

See the reds, the browns, the golds,
As autumn glory here unfolds.
When each year nature paves the way;
Tapestry prelude to winter grey.

Ruth Barclay Brook

AWAITING

The deckchairs piled high 'neath canvas,
The refreshment rooms still locked and barred,
The pleasure boats creek at their moorings,
The empty space where donkeys can be hired.
The promenade where countless feet will tread,
Sprawls silent in the early morning sun.

Betty Eileen Houghland

AS WINTER FALLS
(For Louise)

Winter speaks in cold whispers,
As I cry snowflake tears for the broken dreams of yesteryear.

Frosty windows hide from view,
The warm thoughts I still hold for you, which melt the snow.

The icy wind's velvet lips kiss my face,
The source of which there is no trace,
As I look around.

Trudging through the virgin snow,
Unsure of where to go,
As my feet grow numb.

Cold sunlight plays upon my eyes,
A vision of you which slowly dies,
But I can still smile.

Dreaming of forbidden shores,
Where all that's mine is also yours,
But the cold wind blows.

And now I know this sorrow I feel will never heal,
As like myself, the winter falls.

I call out your name,
But it drifts way unheard.

I tell myself, some day soon. . .
But I don't believe a word.

Stuart Ewen

I SIT! I STARE!

With pen in hand, I sit, I stare.
The medium below is naked, still bare.

> I think of things that should have been,
> and even some that were.
> I think of things that could well be.
> May the best still occur!

I remember well so many years gone by,
with recent events forgot, no matter how I try.
The clarity of old lives on without illusion
but yesterday's events are littered in confusion.

I close my eyes to look inside
what wonders does the grey matter hide?
Whirls, twirls, multi-coloured Catherine wheels
stars hither and thither turning upon their heels.
Such visualities are background of no concern
there is something within I must discern.

> The fruition of thought is a deliberate task
> the earthiness of this is all I ask.
> Something to grasp, to utilise,
> within oneself one is ever wise.

I look, I see, I know it's there,
to bring it forth is all I care.
That is a step beyond my wildest dreams.
Yet one must try, or so it seems.

M G Bradley

BREAKING UP

May the meeting come soon
To make an end to uncertainty.
After I will accept the separation,
My mind will be at rest.
But many questions need an answer
To create an understanding before we part.

Perhaps now there be an openness
Now ties are broken, freedom is yours.
Only rarely did you unlock your thoughts
To show the real person. Usually your mask,
Silken soft, adopted to shield, remained impervious
Though I had not caused its donning.

Always your going left frustration.
Frustration because you would not remove it,
Would not cast off its anonymity.
I only knew the assumed persona.
How you had cocooned yourself against
The situation. But now you are free.
Will you come to this final meeting
The real person or must we maintain this charade?

Marguerite F Wilkinson

BLOWN IN FROM CHICAGO

It's often hard to get going,
especially when you've
been out of the country,
out of your clothes, and just
generally
out of circulation.

Who gives a damn
what happens next?
Just
drink
after drink after
drink.

Rutted roads that wind over
mountains and look down
upon American-made windmills.
My
volcanic eyes burn.
Where do you start looking,
and what do you want to see anyhow?

And my body shudders with fits of coughing.
4 a.m. on a makeshift
sofa-bed, as a cockroach rattles the chain on
the bath-plug, trying and trying again to
climb up out of the tub.

Built to last.
Whilst the cement falls out from between the
breeze-block walls and the cacti reach
for dew and the sand blows across
the road.

And although it's bound to run out some time,
for now, at least,
the money and the beer
are in good supply.

P Hope

INSOMNIA

In the shadows of my dreams
I feel your presence
sneak into my mind.
Every footstep -
the pumping of adrenaline as you near.
Your silhouette dances
against my eyelids.
A cry escapes as I
drown within my tears.

Ann Moffat

THE SPOILS OF WAR

It all happened in a split-second,
A simple heartbeat,
A single breath:
Time trapped in suspension.
A loud retort resounded, reminiscent of the car accident he'd suffered
    and survived several years before.
Then silence.
The CO's order,
And he ran
With the others.
The outpost razed, the enemy fire doused,
And he charged without question
With the others.
Adrenaline surging, mind rejoicing,
He charged.
The enemy routed, the skirmish won,
Honour satisfied.
Later, he strolled among the twisted limbs and splattered guts to claim
    his well-earned trinkets:
A gun, or a flak-jacket,
Or a watch purchased with a peasant's measly wages in some far-off
    foreign land.
Perhaps a gold locket, with a picture of a dead man's wife,
A dead man's kids,
A man like himself, sundered by the orders of others,
By the politics of power and profit,
By a president's megalomaniac ambitions,
By a PM's hypocrisy.
'You've done a good job, lads,' said the CO as the dust and carrion
    settled on the day's end,
And darkness shrouded the graves of many,
But one man's thoughts dwelled on the widows and orphans.

He joined in the drunken revelry, of course,
And laughed at all the right moments,
And joked at all the right moments,
And doused his conscience, like the enemy fire already doused:
The latter to be consigned to the annals of history,
The former to pursue him throughout his life.

Joey McCutheon

MOMENTS . . .

Watching through the window of a darkened room,
Side by side together hear the soundless boom
Of illuminated surf from a dark and velvet sea,
Sparkling in the beauty of reflected panoply,
A thousand twinkling diamonds,
A thousand souls on high,
A thousand, thousand ages in the blinking of an eye.

Early morning footprints in the tide-washed sand,
First love again and back in time as we walk hand in hand
To nowhere in particular, by when we have not planned,
Moments of reflection to renew our friendship and
To fall again in love,
Lost along the lie
Of a thousand, thousand ages in the winking cosmic sky.

Brian J Harrison

A DREAM

It is good you know
That feeling from within
It burns in your stomach
And spreads around your body
It makes you move differently
Makes you let other people see
At last you are smiling - screaming
'Yes - I'm happy with me!'

Joanne Jones

THE LAST WHISPER

The last whisper
What would it be?
A spell of love, a mask of fear,
A twilight sky of perfect peace
A flicker of candlelight in the soft night breeze?
I close my eyes and press to the sand
For one still moment the world is in my hand.
Yet I see myself but still a child
I see no horizon, I see no sun.
But I see a vision of life just begun,
I feel the breeze beneath my wing
I see my place among the spring
The shadow lifts like the salt earth mist
The earth whispers loudly but I cannot speak
for the heart of life the dream I long to seek
Appears before me, a tunnel of light
That guides me along, it shows my path
I'm drawn to it like the light to a moth.
The silence is broken the earth sings its song
The time has come for me to return where I belong.
I open my eyes with a smile
The answer is clear I've touched its power
So fragile and still like life's own flower
I hear now the song it rings through my soul
Its gentle sound has buried its hole
deep within my heart and mind.
A lifelong contract I have signed
Each breath I take, a lifetime I will see
For each passing moment is the last whisper to me.

Sara Baldwin

UNTITLED

When one door closes in time you'll find yourself beside
The entrance to another that beckons you inside
Out of the maze you've wandered through, searching for the way
Making the choices sent to you each and every day
Life isn't neatly labelled 'This Way' or 'Turn Left' or 'Right'
The open door you enter might one day close so tight
The choice is yours to take the chance and go in through the door
Or pass it by and walk along - searching as before
Take every chance life offers you and then one day you'll see
The doors aren't locked - they're only closed - there isn't any key.

Sheila Sleight

LIFE IN A TIN

In granny's fancy button tin are objects round and plural
From dressings of the evenings and suitings of the rural
Buttons from posh shirtings, gold beadings from a purse
Black ovals made for mourning dress, ridings in the hearse
Bows of tartan fastenings from the shoulderings of a dress
Have rememberings for granny, at which I can only guess
There are eyeings from fox-furings in her tin of souvenirs
Buttonings from all over, she's collected down the years
There are precious silver slidings, mixed in with all the rest
Bucklings off old beltings and trimmings off some chest
Snappings from old skirtings can be found in granny's tin
And claspings from old topcoats are also stored within
Embellishings off blousings that have long since had their day
Preserved for further usings in a different sort of way
Ribbonings from the shoes of granny's dancing days
Even old pink lacings from a pair of whalebone stays!
Granny's favourite button is from the greatcoat of my dad
Who died a serving soldier when he was just a 'lad'
Gran's life is in these buttonings, pins 'n' all the others
But there's none of any interest in the tin that is my mother's.

Wendy Gledhill

THOUGHTS

I sit, surrounded by a sea of thought,
Like a ship upon the waves, ideas toss in my head.
A mist engulfs me, cutting me off from the world,
In a trance, I think, drowning and saving thoughts.

Sweet sounds of mermaids, lure
My images from the safety of their crafts.
Tricking me of my thoughts, trying to make me lose my mind,
But determined, I won't let them win.

Submerged in waves, ideas start to drown,
Slip away into the depths of my mind.
Gone, to be lost for ever, until,
I dive in and pull them away from danger.

They toss on the stormy sea of my mind,
A turmoil of images and words.
Waiting, patiently to be found,
Like sailors waiting for their sweethearts.

Pirates attack my mind, stealing my thoughts,
I try to fight them off, make them leave my mind,
But I lose, my thoughts are gone, forgotten.
My ideas die and the sea calms.

Gentle waves lap onto the shore,
Everyday thoughts linger in the shallow waters.
Paddling near the safety of the shore,
Easy to find, not often forgotten.

But somewhere, lurking in the violent storms,
Lie my thoughts, drowning in the deep depths.
One day, I'll save them,
I'll bring them from the waves to the sandy shore,
Of my world.

Ruth Startin

TO-DAY

To-Day is ours for living
Grasp it - if you can -
For Life and time are fleeting,
Gliding softly, swiftly on.

Time is quickly passing,
Slipping through our hands,
Running through our fingers
Like the hot Sahara sands.

So fill each waking moment,
Every second, minute, hour,
Fill them full, to over-flowing,
Let action be your power.

Eagerness will help you
To make *To-Day* worthwhile,
For then you'll find, each inch of time,
Will soon become a mile.

However far you journey,
Whatever length Life's span,
It's each *To-Day* that makes the whole
Of Life's rich golden plan.

Eunice M Caines

TO THE ONE I LOVE

Beneath the air tonight
I breathe a word that cannot be denied
But will the whisper echo right
As my love for you cannot be deprived

In the morning, I breathe a sigh
Relief of pain goes through my vibes
As no answer from you so far
Becomes the silence of my despair

But loving you, is like breaking me
In thousand pieces no human can see
If only time was right
I'd know what to say for life

Amina Patel

THE HEALER

Tell us doctor how do you survive,
Whilst the cat's in the cradle eating you alive,
In the middle of the morning longing for sleep,
When under the covers you wish you could creep,
How do you keep your body together,
When you know your soul's at the end of its tether,
Everybody's pain is before your eyes,
All you wish for is bright blue skies,
Years of study your future moulding,
No end to the burden you are shouldering,
Staring at a computer screen,
Typing up ailments that have been,
Standing besides the hospital bed,
Signing certificates of the dead,
Holding the hand of a terminal child,
Saving the life of one who defiles,
Forgive us for mistaking you for God,
It is in his footsteps you have trod,
So if we imagine you standing tall,
Forgive for forgetting you also fall,
Yours is the very first face we see,
The last one of all when we cease to be.

Linda Bedford

INFORMATION

We hope you have enjoyed reading this book - and that you will continue to enjoy it in the coming years.

If you like reading and writing poetry drop us a line, or give us a call, and we'll send you a free information pack.

Write to :-
Poetry Now Information
1-2 Wainman Road
Woodston
Peterborough
PE2 7BU
(01733) 230746